Lord
You've Been
So Good

A Women's Prayer Journal

Penny L. Sanders

authorHOUSE®

AuthorHouse™
1663 Liberty Drive
Bloomington, IN 47403
www.authorhouse.com
Phone: 833-262-8899

Published by AuthorHouse 07/21/2023

ISBN: 979-8-8230-1166-2 (sc)
ISBN: 979-8-8230-1170-9 (e)

Print information available on the last page.

Foreword

I started my journey with Christ, as a child. Although, it was part of my upbringing to go to church. As I grew older, I realized that I had to make a decision for myself. To have a relationship with the Lord. Not for anyone else. Absorbing, and taking in all the wonderful goodness from him. The Lord wants us to surrender all. There's not a problem too big, or too small that he can't handle. No greater love hath no man than this, that a man lay down his life for his friends. So, I'm going to stand on His promises. It is said, it is hard to come in contact with the Lord. And continue to be the same. There must be a change within us. We want the Lord to guide us, and to keep us. But in order for this to happen. We must choose Him. That's when we truly become aware of his presence. Because, he said, "I knew you before I formed you in your mother's womb. Before you were born I set you apart." Jesus, also said, "I am the way, and the truth, and the life. No one comes to the Father except through me." I've had many challenges in my life, as far as health wise. Having to go through breast cancer twice. It returned after 19 years. I knew that I couldn't handle it on my own. But I wasn't alone. I knew I had to go to God in prayer. I also had my family, friends, loved ones, and Prayer Warriors interceding on my behalf. So, I was able to Praise Him In Advance! I've had many obstacles trying to block my way. But the Lord told me, "To be still and know that I am God." And because of my faith in Him, "I'm Still Here." So I can testify of His goodness, and all He's done for me. He is my Lord, and Saviour! For I know that I am a Living, Walking, Testimony. Knowing, he chose me to tell my story. To help others along the way. Because the Lord can use anybody that wants to be used. I know that Jesus is the best thing that ever happened to me. Romans 8:31 says, "She who kneels before God can stand before anyone." We are called victorious by our testimony. I created this journal for women to encourage, and lift one another up. Hopefully for someone to be healed. To be set free from whatever is burdening you. Just to hold on, and keep the faith. I want you to know my journey getting here wasn't easy. Everyone's journey is different. You talk to the Lord, and tell your story. Because no one can tell your story like you. Making that personal connection. That one on one. The Lord treasures that time with you. Telling Him, your innermost thoughts. In the midnight hour, when you can't talk to anyone else. Because every tear you cry he knows all about it. He will wipe all your tears away. Weeping may endure for a night, but joy cometh in the morning. There is a blessing in the storm. We are all work in progress, like Highway signs. Hold to God's unchanging hand. Let's get excited in the Lord. Never lacking in zeal, but keep your spiritual fervor, serving the Lord. Be Blessed!

Lord, You've been So Good

When I think about your goodness

And all you've done for me.

If I had 10,000 tongues

I would praise you

With every last one.

Lord, you kept me

You've never left me

You've always been by my side.

Lord, you've been so good.

You told me that, you would

Open the floodgates of Heaven,

And pour me out so many blessings

That I wouldn't have enough room

To receive it.

Lord, you've been so good.

You told me to cast

All my cares on you.

For you careth for me.

Rock me in the cradle of your arms,

Reassuring me, you're there.

Lord, you've been so good.

I trust all the plans

You have for me.

Because I know, you know

What's best for me.

Before I was born

You wrote my name in the book of life

My destiny and every little detail.

For you are the author and finisher of our faith.

Even when the nights, seem so long

And I've lost my way.

You never gave up on me.

You're still there,

Lighting the way.

Lord, you've been so good.

Father, I stretch my hands to thee

No other help I know.

If thou withdraw Thyself from me

Wither shall I go.

Lord, I come to you bowed down

On bended knees.

You said, let your requests be known

With a sincere, and open heart.

Look within me

Help me to be the best

That I can be.

Lord, you've been so good.

You asked me, to put my faith in you,

You asked me to be of service to you.

Because I know, you're the King of Kings

And the Lord of Lord's.

You were the chosen one

That came to fulfill, the scripture

For everyone to see.

Lord, you've been so good.

I love that one on one time

We share with one another.

You are definitely, a true friend to me

You understand me.

You love me unconditionally.

Lord, you've been so good.

I put all my trust in you.

Together as a team

We worked it out.

It's all about that still small voice

When I'm listening to what you have to say.

And that comes with obedience,

In following your direction

Every step of the way.

I can truly say,

I don't mind waiting on you, Lord.

Lord, you've been so good.

You were a friend, when I was friendless

You were hope, when I was hopeless.

You were a doctor in the sickroom

And when the doctor, gave me a bad report

You had the final say

For, I believed in your report Lord.

That's why, "I'm Still Here!"

Because you brought me out.

You're a lawyer in the courtroom

And you've never lost a case.

Lord, you've been so good.

The tears, I shed

When I talk to you

In the midnight hour.

Doesn't compare, to the blood you shed

On that old rugged cross,

When you died on Calvary.

No one, could've imagined the pain you felt

For you, to die for our sins, that day.

Crying, Father into thy hands

I commend my spirit.

Lord, you've been so good.

They say, you'll know we're christians by our love

In what we say, and do.

Lord, I'll continue to follow you.

Jesus, just stay with me.

I need you every minute, of every hour.

I need you to cover me

With your blood.

I need you to block

Any weapon that is formed

Against me from the enemy.

But knowing, that me following you,

It comes with the territory.

Lord, you've been so good.

Hide me from myself

When I want to go off

The beaten path.

To help me to do right

When everything around me is going wrong.

Make me better Lord,

I surrender, all.

Your will is what's best for me.

Mold me, shape me, make me

Into the person, I'm meant to be.

Use me as your instrument,

Let me be that vessel,

For all the world to see.

Let me pour out what you poured in.

All of you,

And none of me.

Lord, you've been so good!

Lord You Are Good

Psalm 34:8
O taste and see that the Lord is good: blessed is the man that trusteth in him.

Have You Heard About Jesus

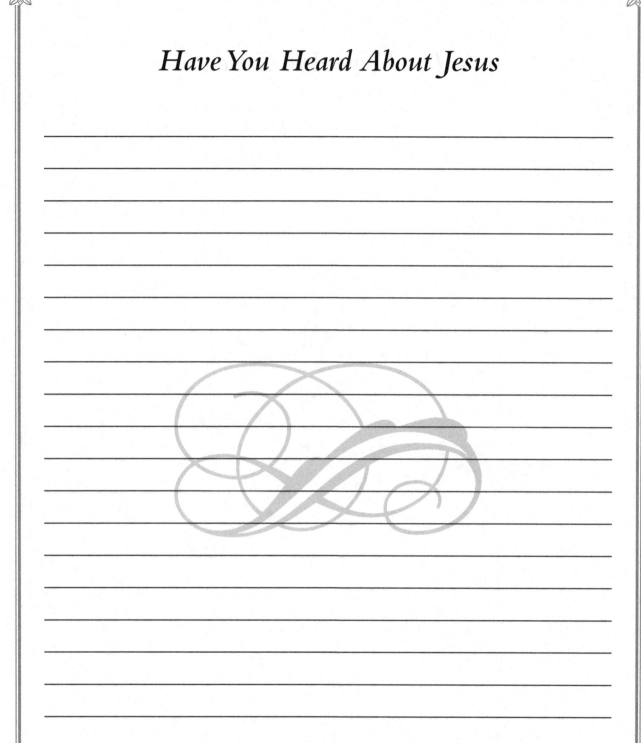

Luke 5:15
*However, the report went around concerning Him all the more; and great
multitudes came together to hear, and to be healed by Him of their infirmities.*

Give Myself Away

Job 22:21
Submit to God, and be at peace with him; in this way prosperity will come to you.

I Can Go To God In Prayer

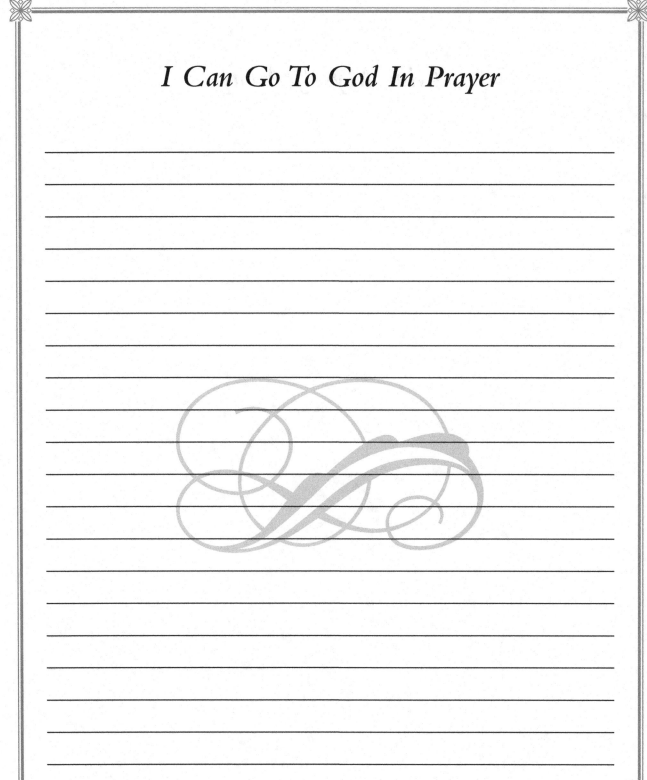

Mark 11:24
Therefore I say unto you, What things soever ye desire when ye pray, believe that ye receive them, and ye shall have them.

I Believe

Hebrews 11:1
Now faith is the substance of things hoped for, the evidence of things not seen.

Encourage Yourself

Psalm 121:1-2
1) I will lift up mine eyes unto the hills, from whence cometh my help.
2) My help cometh from the Lord, which made heaven and earth.

You Spoke Over Me

Jeremiah 29:11
For I know the plans I have for you, declares the Lord, plans for
welfare and not for evil, to give you a future and a hope.

Something About That Name

Phillippians 2:9-10
9) Wherefore God also hath highly exalted him, and
given him a name which is above every name.
10) That at the name of Jesus every knee should bow, of things in
heaven, and things in earth, and things under the earth.

I Told The Storm

Mark 4:39
And he arose and rebuked the wind, and said unto the sea, Peace
be still. And the wind ceased, and there was a great calm.

Forever At Your Feet

Psalm 119:105
Your word is a lamp to my feet and a light to my path.

Miracles, Signs, & Wonders

Acts 4:30
By stretching forth thine hand to heal; and that signs and wonders
may be done by the name of thy holy child Jesus.

Better Days

Phillippians 4:6-7
"Do not be anxious about anything, but in everything by prayer and supplication with thanksgiving let your requests be made known to God. And the peace of God, which surpasses all understanding, will guard your hearts and your minds in Christ Jesus."

Change Me

2 Corinthians 5:17
Therefore if any man be in Christ, he is a new creature: old
things are passed away; behold, all things become new.

I Trust You

Proverbs 16:3
Commit your work to the Lord and your plans will be established.

No Weapon

Isaiah 54:17
No weapon that is formed against thee shall prosper.

Praise Him In Advance

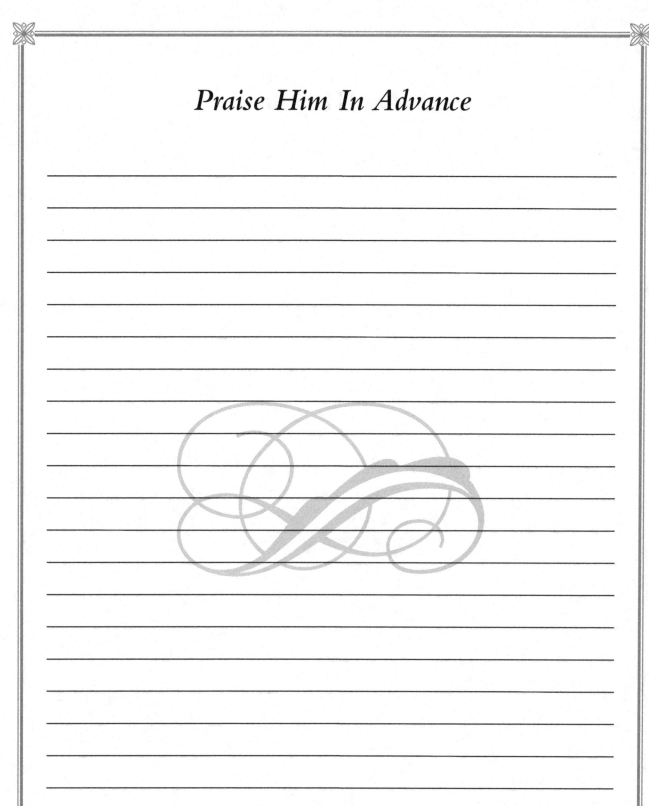

He Knows Your Name

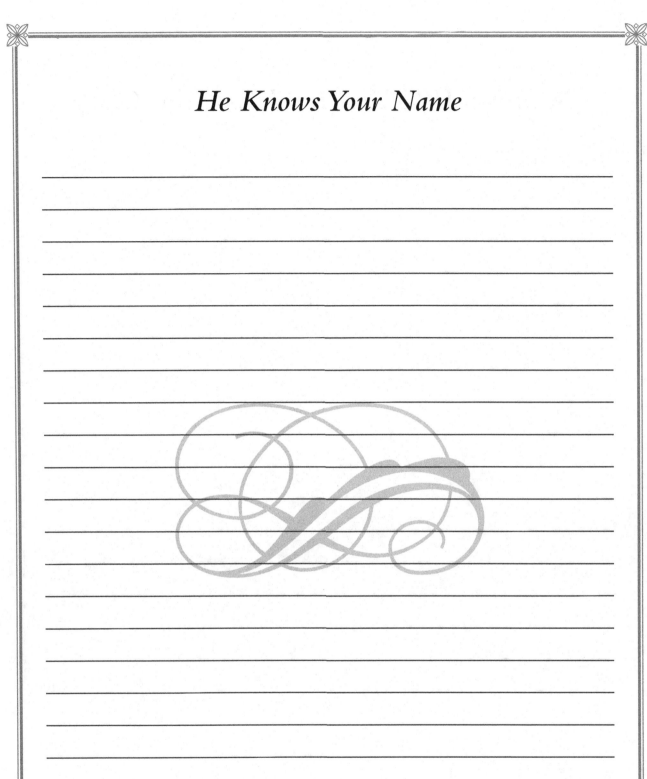

Exodus 33:17
And the Lord said to Moses, "This very thing that you have spoken I will do, for you have found favor in my sight, and I know you by name."

Because of Who You Are, I Give You Glory

_____

_____

_____

_____

_____

_____

_____

_____

_____

_____

_____

_____

_____

_____

_____

_____

_____

_____

Isaiah 25:1
*O Lord, thou art my God; I will exalt thee, I will praise thy name; for thou
hast done wonderful things; thy counsels of old are faithfulness and truth.*

Grateful

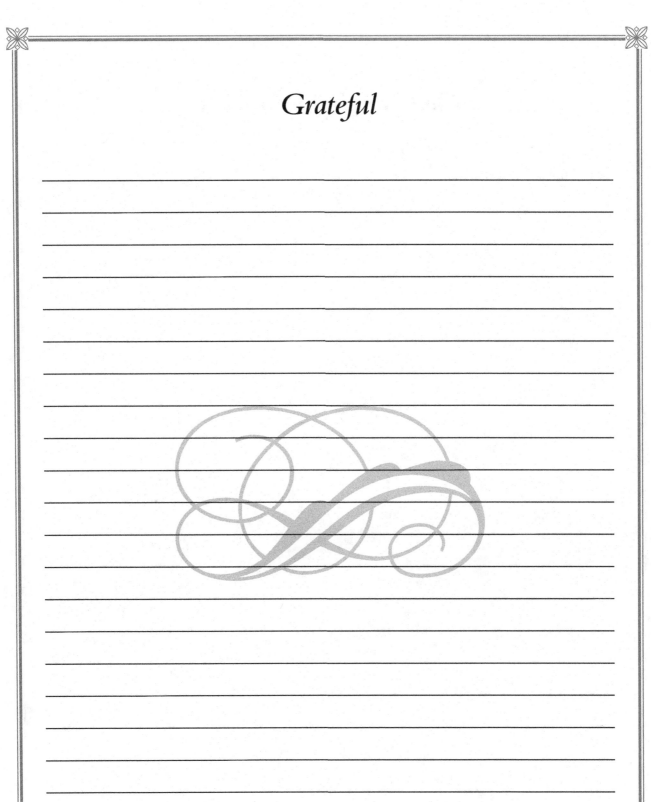

_____
_____
_____
_____
_____
_____
_____
_____
_____
_____
_____
_____
_____
_____
_____
_____
_____
_____
_____
_____

Psalm 106:1
Praise the Lord for he is good; his love endures forever.

God Staying With Us

_____

_____

_____

_____

_____

_____

_____

_____

_____

_____

_____

_____

_____

_____

_____

_____

_____

_____

_____

_____

Mathew 28:20
Teaching them to observe all things whatsoever I have commanded you:
lo I will be with you always even unto the end of the world.

Grace & Mercy

Hebrews 4:16
Let us then approach the throne of grace with confidence, so that we
may receive mercy and find grace to help us in our time of need.

Great is Thy Faithfulness

Be Ye Steadfast

1 Corinthians 15:58

Therefore, my beloved brethren, be ye steadfast, unmoveable, always abounding in the work of the Lord, forasmuch as ye know that your labour is not in vain in the Lord.

God Provides

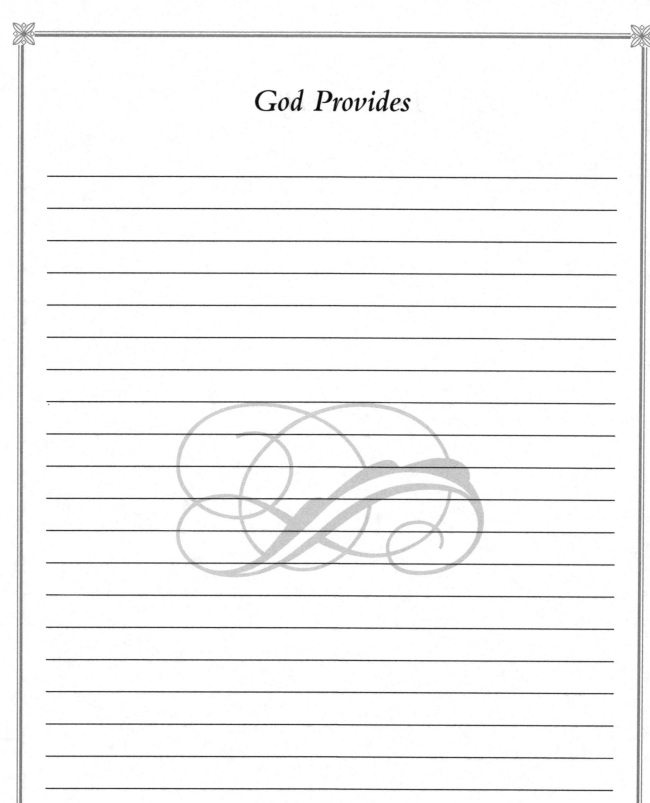

Phillippians 4:19
But my God shall supply all you need according to his riches in glory by Jesus Christ.

How Great Thou Art

You're A Lifter

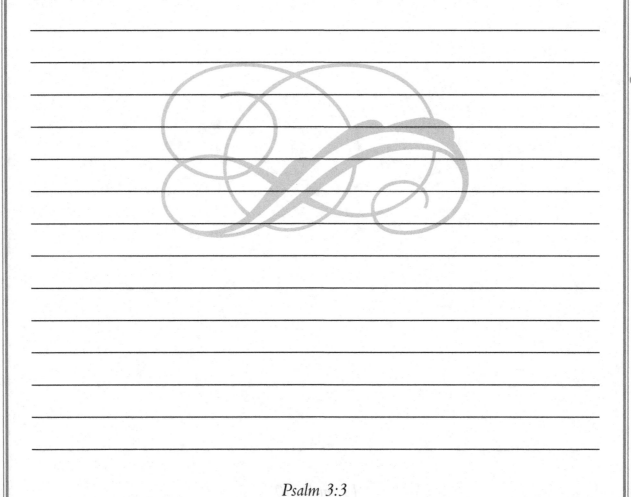

Psalm 3:3
But thou, O Lord, art a shield for me: my glory, and the lifter up of mine head.

Mercy Said No

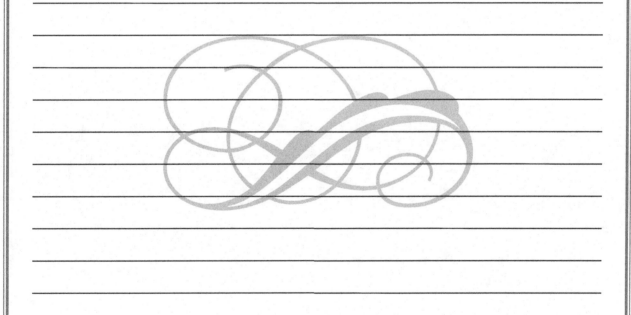

Lamentations 3:22
It is of the Lord's mercies that we are not consumed: His compassion do not fail.

Master Can You Use Me

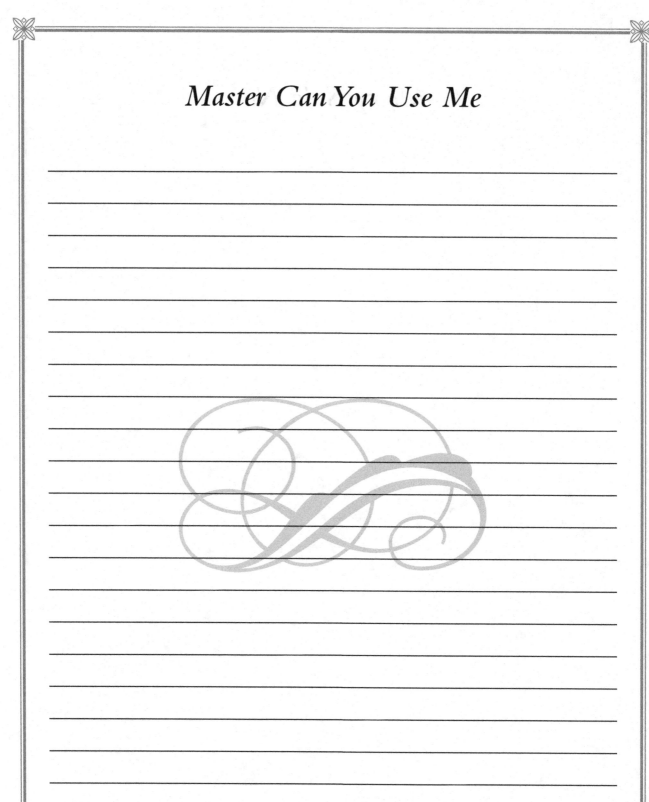

2 Timothy 2:21

If a man therefore purge himself from these, he shall be a vessel unto honour, sanctified, and meet for the master's use, and prepared unto every good work.

Be Healed

Jeremiah 17:14
Heal me, O Lord, and I will be healed; save me and I
will be saved, for you are the one I praise.

God's On Your Side

Psalm 118:6
The Lord is on my side: I will not fear: what can man do unto me.

The Lord Is With Us

Isaiah 41:10
Fear not, for I am with you: be not dismayed, for I am your God; I will strengthen
you, I will help you, I will uphold you with my righteous right hand.

He's Marvelous

Psalm 105:5
Remember his marvelous works that he hath done; his
wonders, and the judgments of his mouth.

Worship Him

John 4:23
*But the hour cometh, and now is, when the true worshippers shall worship the
Father in spirit and in truth: for the Father seeketh such to worship him.*

Finding Peace in the Lord

2 Thessalonians 3:16
Now the Lord of peace himself give you peace always
by all means. The Lord be with you all.

Center of My Joy

John 15:11
These things I have spoken unto you, that my joy might
remain in you, and that your joy might be full.

The Battle is the Lord's

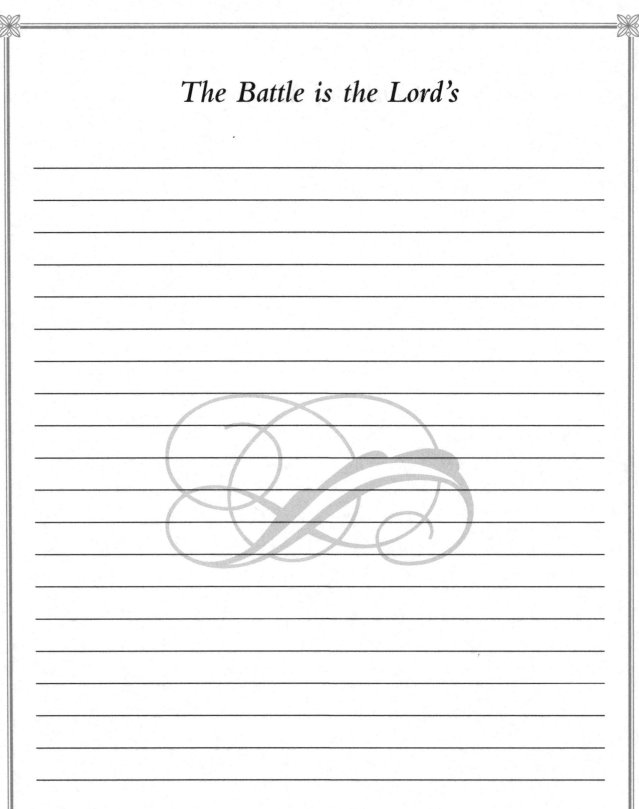

2 Chronicles 20:15
And he said, Hearken ye, all Judah, and ye inhabitants of Jerusalem, and thou
king Jehoshaphat, Thus saith the Lord unto you, Be not afraid nor dismayed
by reason of this great multitude; for the battle is not yours, but God's.

Thank You For It All

Psalm 107:21
Let them give thanks to the Lord for his unfailing love
and his wonderful deeds for mankind.

He Chose Me

Deuteronomy 14:2

For you are a people holy to the Lord your God, and the Lord has chosen you to be a people for his treasured possession, out of all the peoples who are on the face of the earth.

Stir Up The Gift

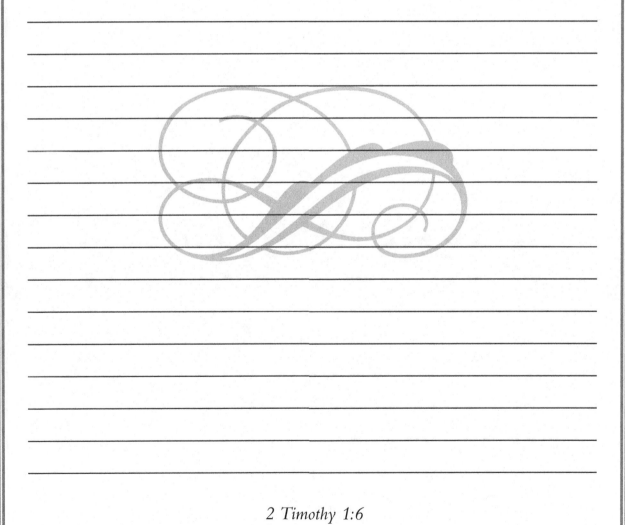

2 Timothy 1:6
Wherefore I put thee in remembrance that thou stir up the gift of
God, which is in thee by the putting on of my hands.

God's Unchanging Hand

Malachi 3:6
For I am the Lord, I change not.

Jehovah Jireh

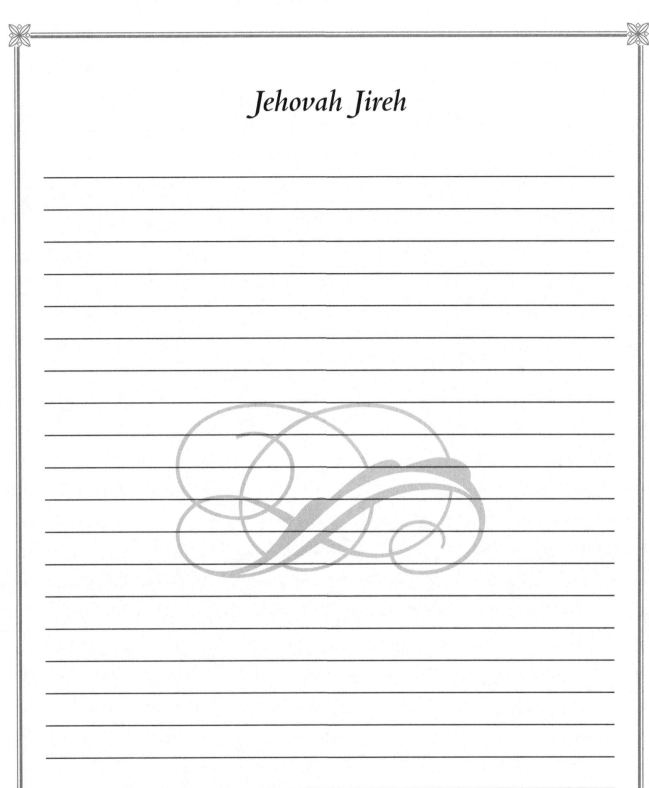

Genesis 22:14
And Abraham called the name of the place, The-LORD-Will-Provide; as it is said to this day, "In the Mount of the LORD it shall be provided."

Jehovah Shalom

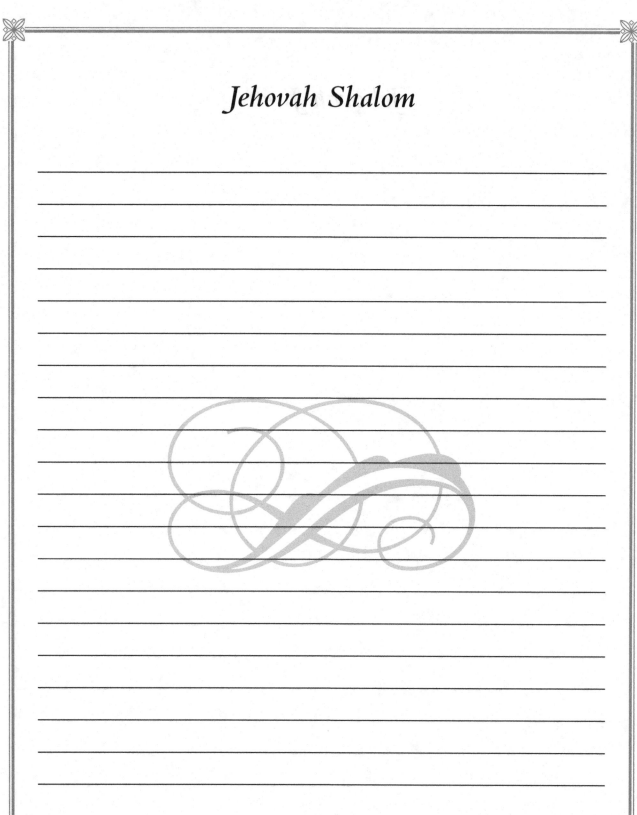

Judges 6:24
Then Gideon built an altar there to the Lord and named it The Lord is Peace. To this day it is still in Ophrah of the Abiezrites.

Jehovah Nissi

Exodus 17:15
And Moses built an altar, and called the name of it
Jehovahnissi (that is, The Lord is my banner).

Jehovah Rapha

Exodus 15:26
He said, if you will listen carefully to the voice of the Lord your God
and do what is right in his sight, obeying his commands and keeping
all his decrees, then I will not make you suffer any of the diseases I
sent on the Egyptians; for I am the Lord who heals you.

50

Make Me Better

Ephesians 2:10
*For we are God's handiwork, created in Christ Jesus to do good
works, which God prepared in advance for us to do.*

Determined To Follow Jesus

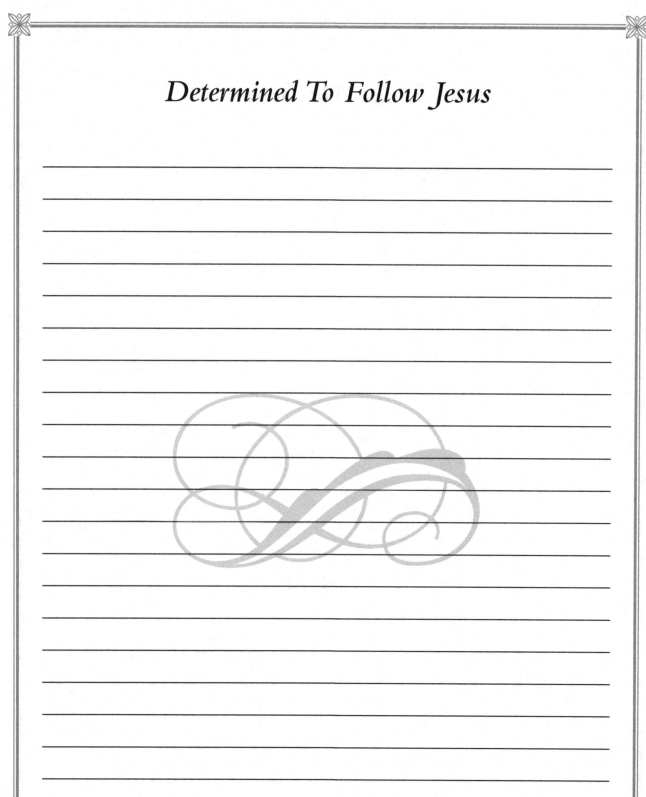

Mathew 16:24
Then Jesus told his disciples, if anyone would come after me, let
him deny himself and take up his cross and follow me.

Blessed Assurance

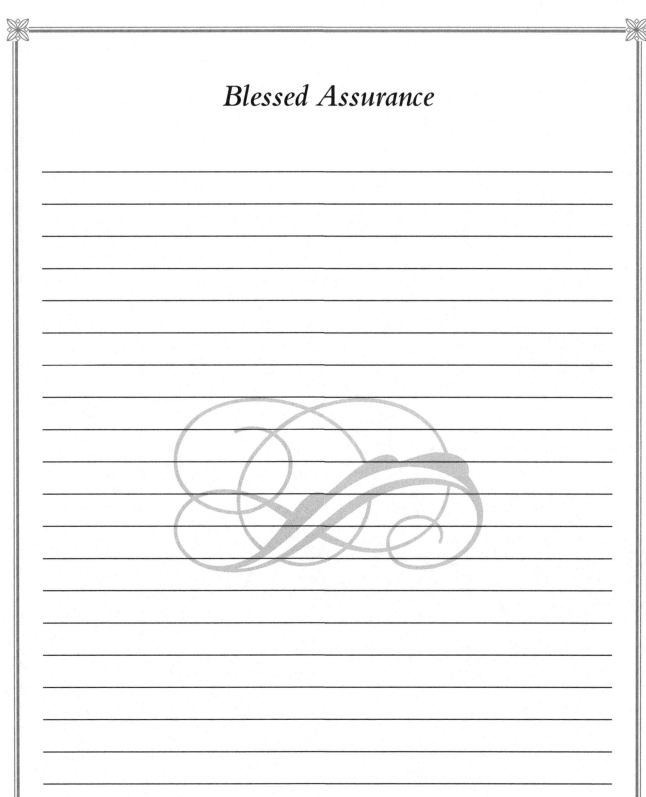

Hebrews 10:22
Let us draw near with a true heart in full assurance of faith, having our hearts
sprinkled from an evil conscience and our bodies washed with pure heart.

Never Lost A Battle

Deuteronomy 20:4
For the Lord your God is the one who goes with you, to
fight for you against your enemies to save you.

He Saw The Best In Me

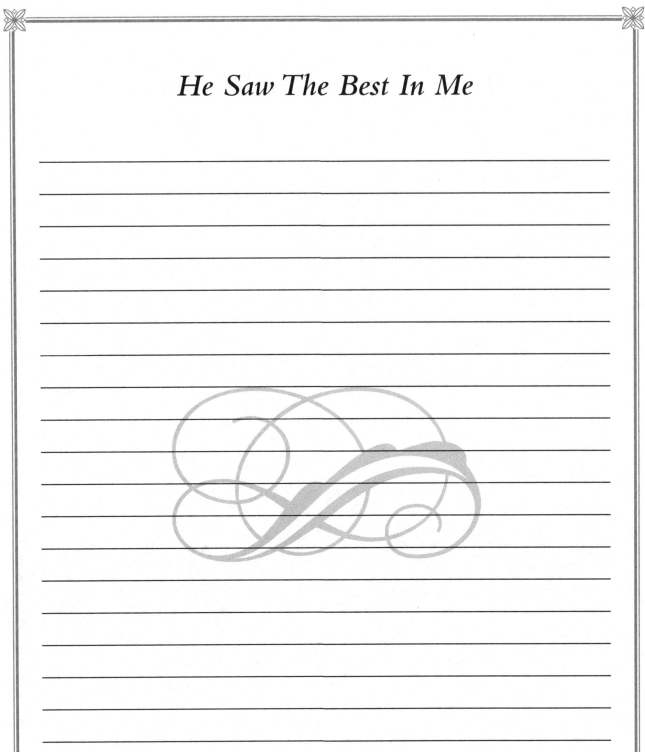

Jeremiah 12:3
But you, O Lord, know me; you see me, and test my heart toward you.

His Eye Is On The Sparrow

Mathew 6:26
*Look at the birds of the air; they neither sow, nor reap, nor gather into barns, and
yet your Heavenly Father feeds them. Are you not of more value than they?*

Walk Into Your Destiny

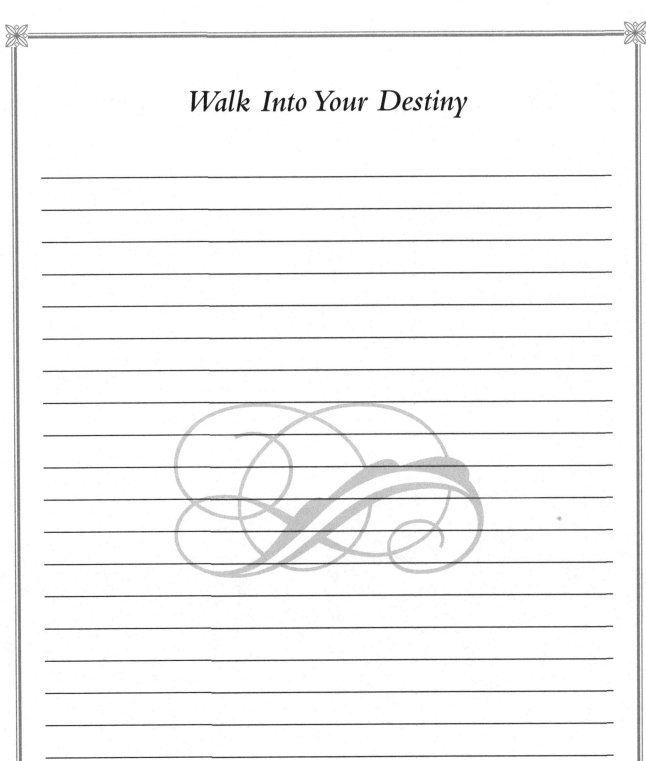

Jeremiah 1:5
*Before I formed you in the womb I knew you, before you were born
I set you apart; I appointed you as a prophet to the nations.*

It's Not Over-Until God Says It's Over

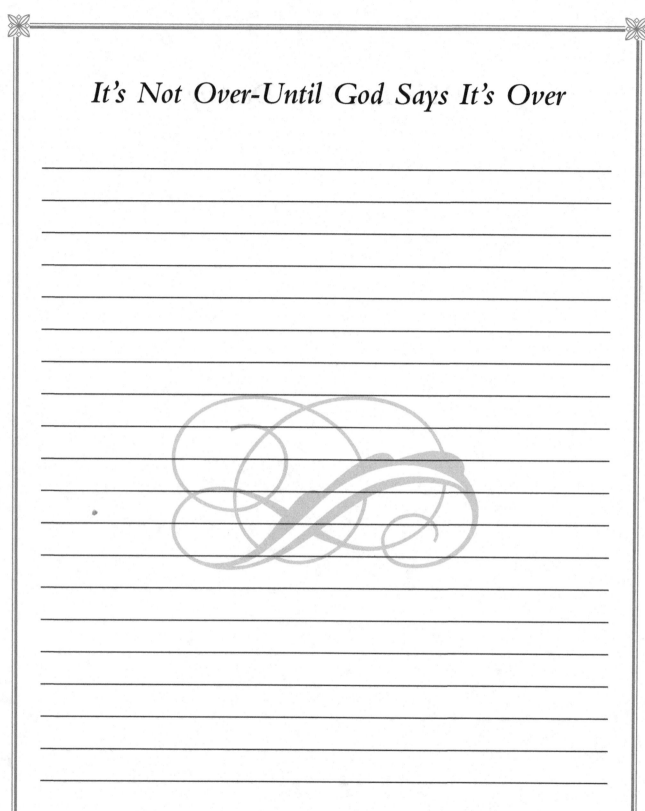

Jeremiah 29:11
For I know the plans I have for you, declares the Lord, plans
for welfare and not evil, to give you a future and hope

Let Not Your Heart Be Troubled

John 14:1
Let not your heart be troubled: ye believe in God, believe also in me.

I Go To Prepare A Place

Exodus 23:20
Behold, I send an Angel before thee, to keep thee in the way,
and to bring thee into the place which I have prepared.

Weeping May Endure For A Night

Psalm 30:5
Weeping may endure for a night, but joy cometh in the morning.

Touch Not My Annointed

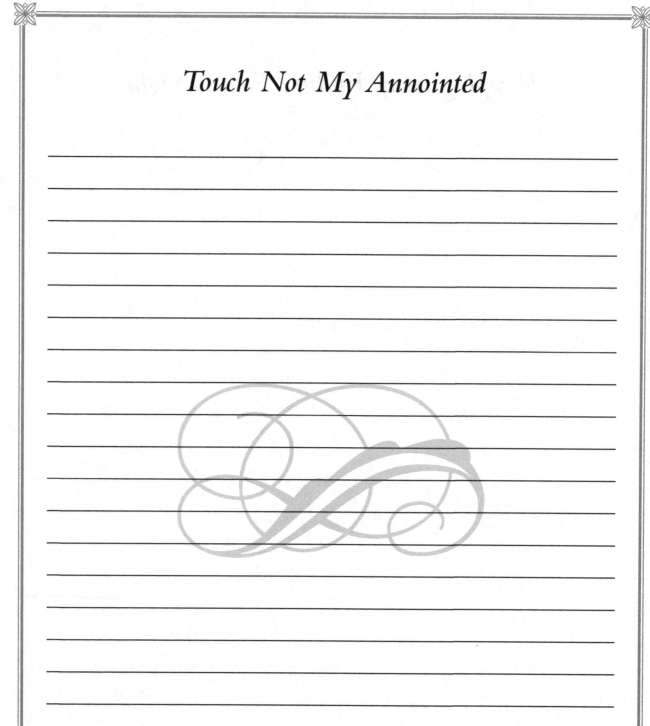

God Is Our Refuge

Psalm 46:1
God is our refuge and strength, a very present help in trouble.

Overcome by Our Testimony

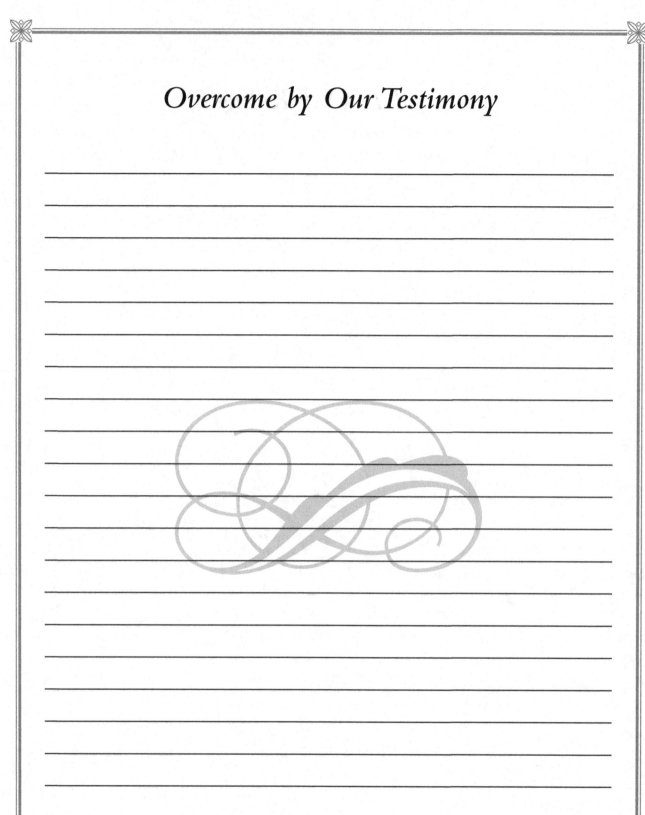

The Lord Is My Shepherd

Psalm 23
The Lord is my shepherd: I shall not want.

Whole Armor Of God

Ephesians 6:11
Put on the whole armour of God, that ye may be able
to stand against the wiles of the devil.

Not By Might

Zechariah 4:6
So he said to me, This is the word of the Lord to Zerubbabel:Not by might nor by power, but by my spirit, says the Lord almighty.

The Lord Is My Rock

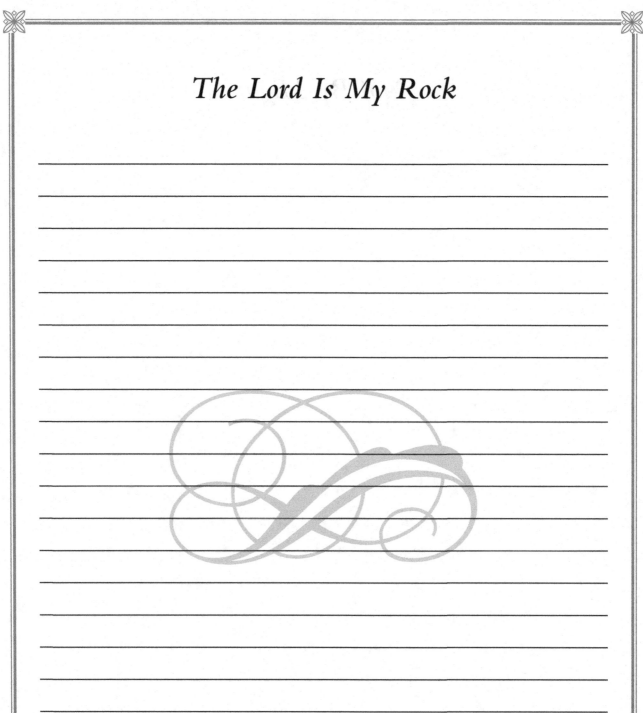

Psalm 18:2
The Lord is my rock and my fortress and my deliverer, my God, my rock in whom I take refuge, my shield, and the horn of my salvation, my stronghold.

Testing of Your Faith

James 1:2
Count it all joy, my brothers, when you meet trials of various kinds.

Flood Gates of Heaven

_____

_____

_____

_____

_____

_____

_____

_____

_____

_____

_____

_____

_____

_____

_____

_____

_____

_____

_____

Malachi 3:10
Bring the whole tithe into the storehouse, that there may be food in my house. Test me in this; says the Lord Almighty, and see if I will not throw open the floodgates of heaven and pour out so much blessing that there will not be room enough to receive it.

God Is For Us

Romans 8:31
If God is for us, who can be against us.

No Greater Love

John 15:13
Greater love hath no man than this, that a man lay down his life for his friends.

Meditate on these Things

Finally, brethren, whatever things are true, whatever things are noble, whatever things are just, whatever things are pure, whatever things are lovely, whatever things are of good report, if there is any virtue, and if there be any praise, think on these things.

Order My Steps

Psalm 37:23
The steps of a good man are ordered by the Lord: and he delighteth in his way.

The Lord Is My Light

Psalm 27:1
The Lord is my light and my salvation, whom shall I fear? The Lord is the strength of my life; Of whom shall I be afraid.

Please Be Patient With Me

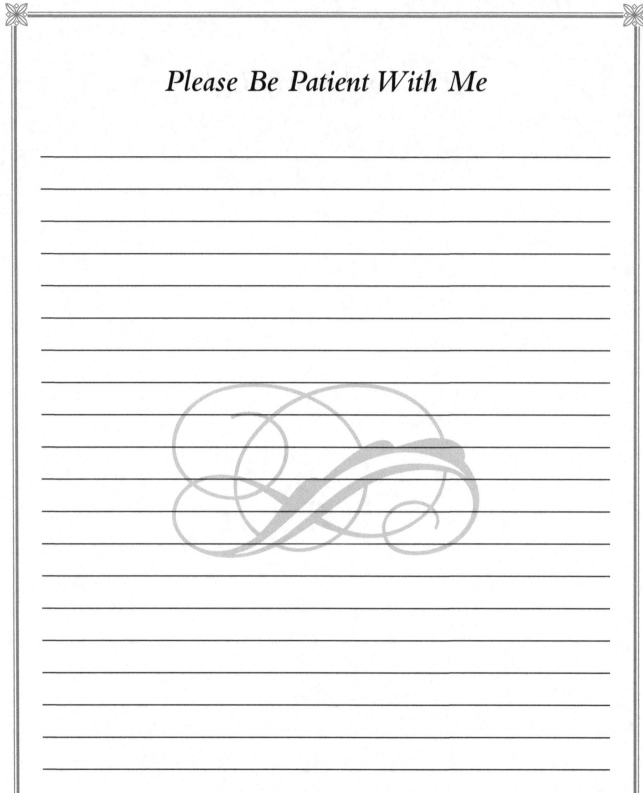

Psalm 86:15
*But You, O Lord, are a God merciful and gracious. Slow to
anger and abundant in loving kindness and truth.*

He's Working It Out In Your Favor

Romans 8:28
*And we know that all things work together for good to them that
love God, to them who are called according to his purposes.*

We Shall Behold Him

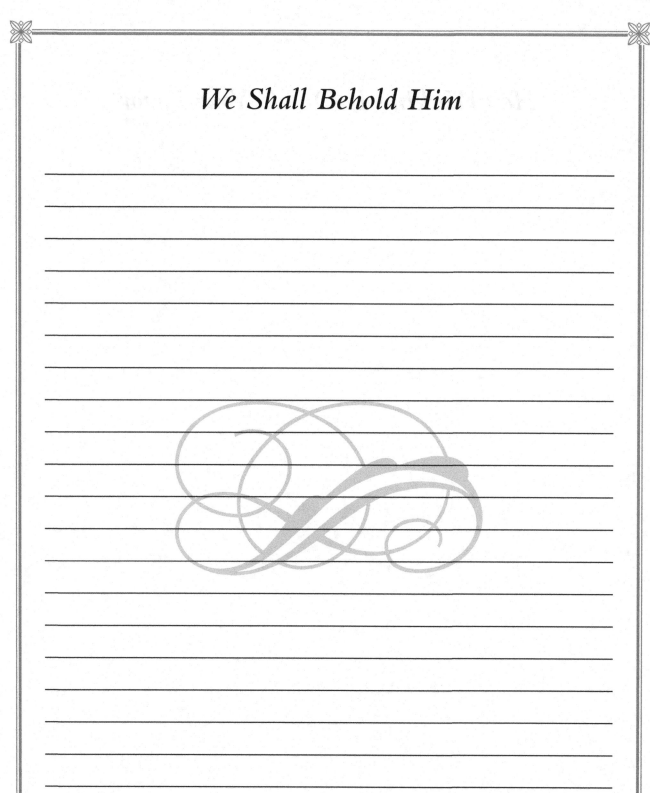

1 John 3:2
Beloved, we are now children of God, and what we will be has not
yet been made known. But we know that when Christ appears
we shall be like him, for we shall see him as he is.

He's Marvelous

Psalm 118:23
This is the Lord's doing:it is marvellous in our eyes.

Be Ye Also Ready

Mathew 24:44
Therefore be ye also ready: for in such an hour as ye think not the Son of man cometh.

Greater Is Coming

John 14:12
Truly, truly, I say to you, whoever believes in me will also do the works that I do; and greater works than these will he do, because I am going to the Father.

I Don't Mind Waiting on the Lord

Psalm 27:14
Wait on the Lord: be of good courage, and he shall
strengthen thine heart: wait, I say, on the Lord.

82

I Rest In You

Psalm 62:1
Truly my soul finds rest in God; my salvation come from him.

When He Speaks

Genesis 1:14
Then God said, "Let there be lights in the expanse of the heavens to separate the day from night, and let them be for signs and for seasons and for days and years.

Breaking of Day

Genesis 32:26
Then he said, "Let me go, for the dawn is breaking." But he
said, "I will not let you go unless you bless me."

85

Mary Don't You Weep

John 20:11-12
11) Now Mary stood outside the tomb crying. As she wept, she bent over
to look into the tomb. 12) and saw two angels in white, seated where
Jesus' body had been, one at the head and the other at the foot.

They that Wait

But they wait upon the Lord shall renew their strength; they shall mount up with wings as eagles; they shall run, and not be weary; and they shall walk, and not faint.

Safe In His Arms

Proverbs 18:10
The name of the Lord is a strong tower, the righteous run to it and are safe.

I Can Do All Things Through Christ

Phillippians 4:13
I can do all things through Christ which strengtheneth me.

Holy Is The Lamb

John 1:29
The next day John saw Jesus coming toward him and said, "Look,
the lamb of God, who takes away the sin of the world."

Precious Lord

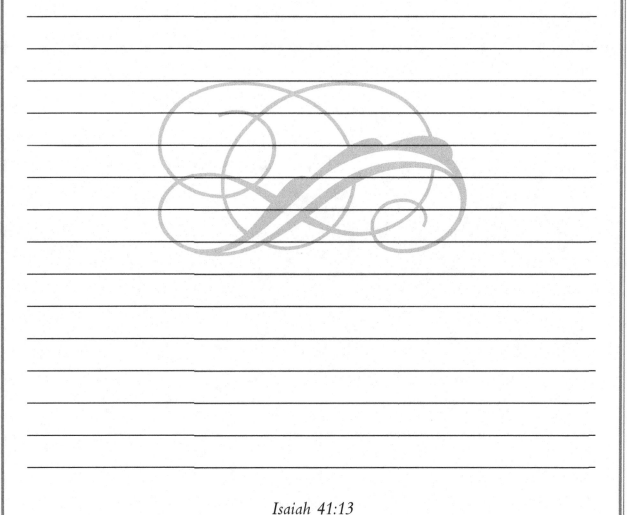

Isaiah 41:13
*For the Lord your God, hold your right hand; it is I
who say to you, fear not, I will help you.*

Faith That Conquers

1 John 5:4
For everyone who has been born of God overcomes the world.
And this is the victory that has overcome the world-our faith.

Train Up a Child

Proverbs 22:6
Train up a child in the way he should go; even when he is old he will not depart from it.

Thank God For My Mansion

John 14:2
In my Father's house are many mansions: if it were not so,
I would have told you. I go to prepare a place for you.

Because He Lives

John 14:19

A little while longer and the world will see me no more, but
you will see me. Because I live, you will live also.

12 Gates to the City

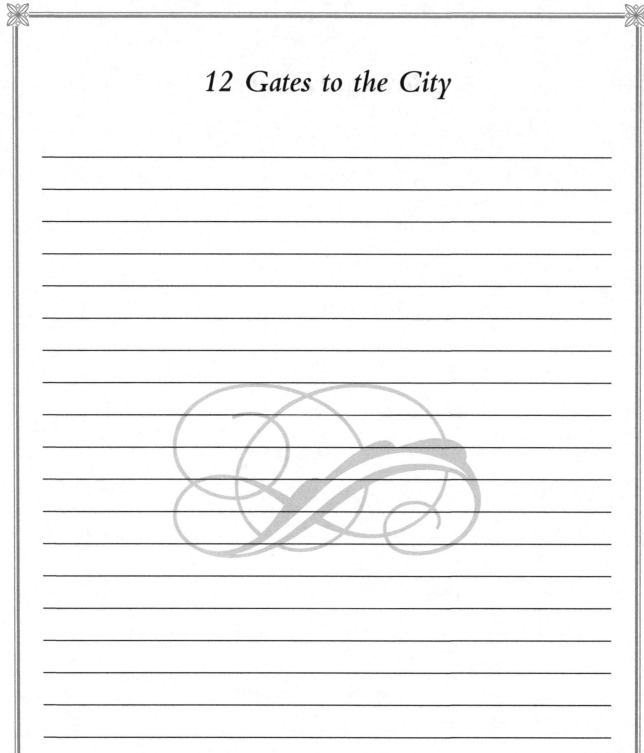

Revelation 2:12
The city had a great and high wall with twelve gates inscribed with
the twelve tribes of Israel, and twelve angels at the gates.

Never Lose Your Praise

Psalm 68:3
But may the righteous be glad and rejoice before God; may they be happy and joyful.

Holy One

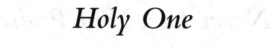

Isaiah 43:3
For I am the Lord, your God, the Holy One of Israel, your Savior.

One Day in Paradise

Luke 23; 42-43
42) And he said unto Jesus, Lord, remember me when thou comest into the kingdom. 43) And Jesus said unto him, Verily I say unto thee, To day shalt thou be with me in paradise.

Everyday is a Day of Thanksgiving

1 Thessalonians 5:16-18
16) Rejoice evermore. 17) Pray without ceasing. 18) In everything give
thanks: this is the will of God in Christ Jesus concerning you.

100

Passing Out Blessings

Mathew 6:33
But seek first the kingdom of God and his righteousness,
and all these things will be added to you.

Where is Your Faith

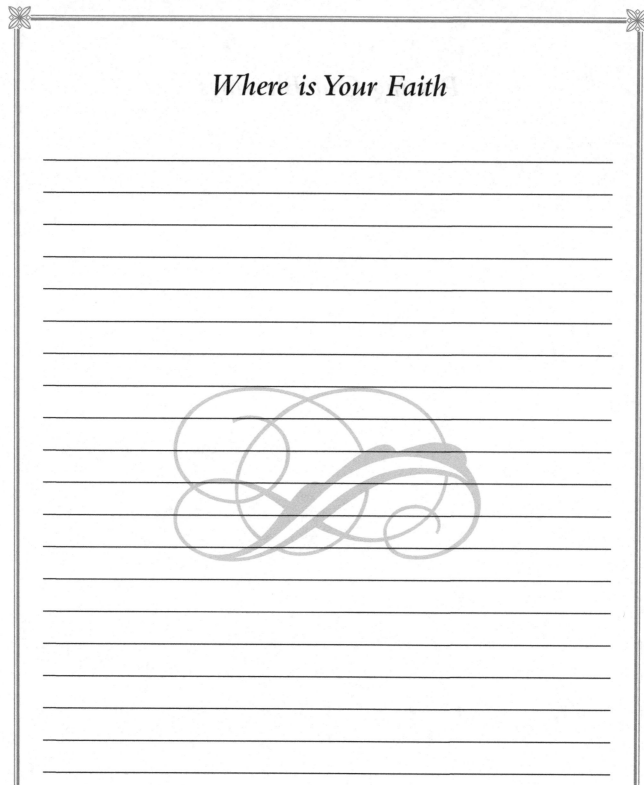

_____

_____

_____

_____

_____

_____

_____

_____

_____

_____

_____

_____

_____

_____

_____

_____

_____

_____

Mathew 17:20
So Jesus said to them, Because of your unbelief: for assuredly, I say to you,
if you have faith as a mustard seed, you will say to the mountain, move from
here to there, and it will move; and nothing will be impossible for you.

I Love The Lord

Luke 10:27
And he answering said, Thou shalt love the Lord thy God with all thy heart, and with all thy soul, and with all thy strength, and all thy mind; and thy neighbor as thyself

Till We Meet Again

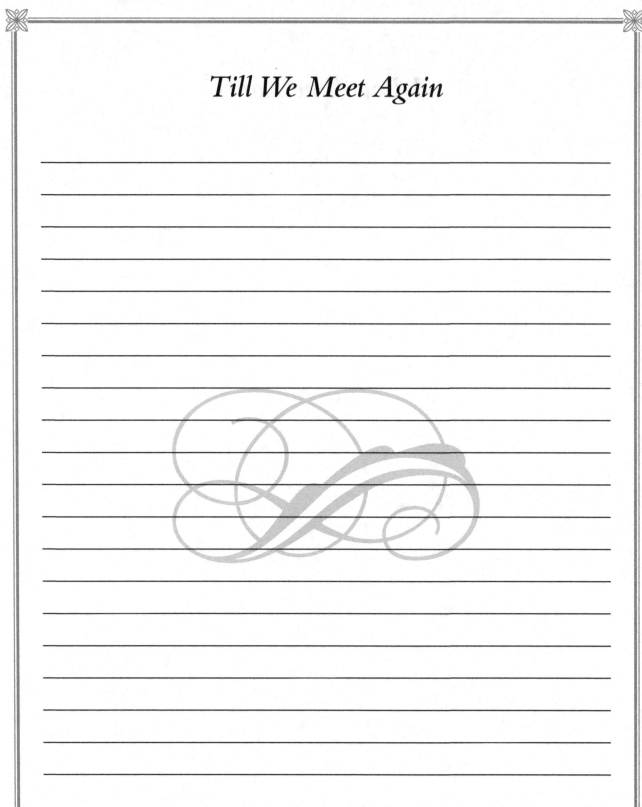

2 Peter 3:13
*But according to his promise we are waiting for new heavens
and a new earth in which righteousness dwells.*

Upon This Rock

Mathew 16:18
And I say unto thee, That thou art Peter, and upon this rock I will
build my church; and the gates of hell shall not prevail against it.

The Lost Sheep

4) Suppose one of you had a hundred sheep and loses one of them. Doesn't he leave the ninety-nine in the open country and go after the lost sheep until he finds it? 5) And when he finds it, he joyfully puts it on his shoulders 6) and goes. Then he calls his friends and neighbors together and says, "Rejoice with me; I have found my lost sheep." 7) I tell you that in the same way there will be more rejoicing in heaven over one sinner who repents than over ninety-nine righteous persons who do not need to repent.

Lord, I Need A Word from You

Lord, I'm down here

Waiting for a word from You.

I've cried, many tears

But, I'm still waiting for a word from You.

You said, "When praises go up

Blessings come down."

I'm waiting for a word from You.

You said, all I need is the

"Faith, the size of a mustard seed."

And, "I can say to the mountain

Move from here to there."

And it will move.

For there is nothing impossible, for You!

I'm waiting for a word from You.

While still, in my Mothers womb

You had a plan for my life.

That's why I'm so Grateful!

Lord, I'm waiting for a word from You.

Sometimes, You have to hide me from myself.

Of self doubt,

From crying at night.

When no one is listening, but You.

For letting the enemy, enter my mind

And thinking, I won't make it through.

Knowing, You already said it

It's already done!

Lord, I need a word from You.

My heart, my mind, and my soul says

Oh, but God!

You delivered Abraham, Isaac, and Jacob

To the Promised Land.

Lord, I need a word from You.

Touch me, like you did before

For you're a God, of an Encore!

You had Moses, to lead your people

Out of Egypt.

You parted the Red Sea.

You performed, miracle after miracle.

Lord, I just need a word from You.

Jehovah Shalom, Lord You are my peace.

Jehovah Raha, Lord You are my Shepherd.

Jehovah Jireh, I know You will provide.

Jehovah Nissi, Lord You are my banner.

Jehovah Tsidkenu, Lord You are righteous.

Jehovah Shammah, Lord You are with me.

Jehovah Rapha, You are my healer!

You are Omnipotent, with all power.

Your Omnipresence surrounds me at all times.

Lord, just a word from You.

For each pool of Bethesda,

I need your Healing!

I need Restoration, each and every day!

I need Breakthrough, from anything that's not like You!

I need Deliverance, cleanse me Lord!

I need Salvation, so I can stand in your Presence!

I need all these things,

So, I can Be Made Whole!

Lord, I need a word from You.

Bind, all these illnesses

That keeps coming in my life.

I Declare, and Decree

I shall be set free!

I claim Victory, In Your Name!

Because of my willingness to serve You,

"No weapon that is formed against thee shall prosper."

The enemy didn't know, who I was

When he kept trying to attack me.

Not only who I was,

But, whose I was.

For You kept me

Because, I am your child.

And you would never fail me.

Lord, I need a word from You.

You carried that Old Rugged Cross.

They whipped You, all night.long.

They put a Crown of Thorns, on your head

Mimicking, You were the King of the Jews.

They hung You high on that cross.

They nailed your hands and feet.

They pierced you, in your side Lord

The blood came streaming down.

Oh, what a Sacrifice!

The sky grew dark, and covered the land.

Just knowing that You

Did that for me.

I can't help, but Praise Your Holy Name!

Your, last three words

"It is Finished!"

Those are the words,

That I needed You.

Nothing else needs to be said.

Thank You Lord!

For those words from You.

In Your Precious Name!

You're Not Welcome here Anymore

When I met you 19 years ago

As a Christian, and follower of Christ.

Jesus said, "If you see a stranger, take them in."

So, I invited you into my home.

I asked, "What would you have of me?"

You told me, you just needed shelter.

Not to worry,

You won't stay long.

You said, "I just want to share some of my things with you."

You told me about a treasure.

That was far from anything

I could possibly imagine.

You tried to mesmerize me,

With your fast talking, and tricks.

I told you, "You really think you're slick."

And when I found out your name

I told you, you must leave.

Because, "Cancer, you're not welcome here anymore!"

I told you, "All you come to do

Is steal, kill, and destroy."

I went down on my knees in prayer.

I asked, Jesus to come help me,

To fight this battle with you.

I held onto my faith,

I knew I had to be strong.

"Cancer, you're not welcome here anymore."

But before you left,

You stole a part of me.

I never thought you would

Come back one day.

I was living my life

Serving a true, and living God.

Trying to be a good, faithful servant.

Believing and depending on His word.

Living my life to the fullest.

Knowing that in life,

You are going to have trials and tribulations.

But, only because our Lord

Has allowed it.

I thought, I wouldn't see you anymore.

But in 2020, you showed up

Back at my door.

I asked, "Haven't you taken enough already?"

You said, "I'm not through with you."

I'm back, to create a little more havoc.

I haven't broken you down

To the point, you can't get back up again.

I'm here to take another part of you.

It wasn't enough, the first go round.

I told you, "That doesn't define me as a person!"

There is so much more to me.

Which undoubtedly, you can't see.

For I am a daughter,

Of the most High King.

You told me, I want to know

"How many more tears can you cry?"

I want to know

"How many more prayers,

Can you call on the Lord for?"

I want to know

"How many Prayer Warriors are on your side?"

"Standing in agreement with you?"

I feel the need to keep attacking you.

Once more, "Cancer, you're not welcome here anymore!"

See, that first time

I wasn't prepared for you.

I only had one doctor to battle you.

But now, I have a whole team

Who are good at what they do.

I put on the full armor of God

So, I can take a stand against you.

In Ephesians 6:13-17 says

Therefore put on the full armor of God,

So that when the day of evil comes,

You may be able to stand your ground

And after you have done everything, to stand.

Stand firm then, with the belt of truth

Buckled around your waist,

With the breastplate of righteousness in place,

And with your feet fitted with the

Readiness that comes from the gospel of peace.

In addition to all this, take up the shield of faith,

With which you can extinguish all

The flaming arrows of the evil one.

Take the helmet of salvation

And the sword of the Spirit,

Which is the word of God.

"Cancer, you're not welcome here anymore!"

You cannot win against my God!

Outward appearances don't mean anything

Can you see this heart that's within me?

These changes are only temporary.

I have so many people, who love me

Then you can even begin to imagine.

And with my testimony

I will have a lot more.

You got to go, by the power of the Holy Ghost!

Get out of my house,

Get out of my body.

"Cancer, you're not welcome here anymore!"

Because you didn't pay attention

To the mustard seed,

That was at my front door!

Penny L. Sanders

Printed in the United States
by Baker & Taylor Publisher Services